I Want A Pet Tortoise

Gail Forsyth

This publication has been researched and designed to provide accurate pet care, while helping children learn the responsibilities that entail having to care for their pet tortoise.

No part of this book is to be copied without written permission from the publisher and author.

Breed Profiles Publishing
Cedar City, UT 84721

Table of Contents

Note To Parents From The Author   1
Acknowledgment   2
My Pledge   3
Personal Page For Your Tortoise   4
Always Wash Your Hands   5
General Information on Tortoises   6
Door Hanger   9
Questions and Answers   11
Word Find   12
My Shell   13
Color Me   14
Draw Me A Shell   15
My Pen   16
Substrate   18
Lighting   19
Healthy Foods For Tortoises   20
What Not To Feed Your Tortoise   22
Vitamins & Minerals   23
Questions and Answers on Food   24
Soaking   25
Tort Table   26
Group of 5 Tortoises to Color   27
Taking Your Tortoise Outdoors   28
Tortoise Maze   29
Draw Some Scutes   30
Hibernation   31
Captive Bred Tortoises   32
Health Issues For Tortoises   33
Missing Vowels   34
Word Find   35
Color Me   36
Daily Care Chart   37
Make Your Own Note Cards   38
Make Your Own Bookmark   41
Other Books in the Series   43

Note To Parents From The Author

As a parent and grandparent myself, I know the cries and wants of a child that desires a pet. When I was a child I had the same wishes to obtain just about every kind of pet I could. Every book I bought or checked out at the library was pet or animal related.

If your child has been asking for a tortoise, only you know if he or she is ready to take on that commitment. Your supervision will ensure that the pet is being well cared for and you'll be pleased with watching your child learn to care and nurture a pet. They may even grow up to follow a career in the pet field.

Tortoises can be a good choice for children. They don't require a lot of care, or any special licenses or tend to bite the mailman.

You'll find this book will help your child learn about the needs of their tortoise and all the while having a fun time doing it. The book has basic care topics that your child can read, plus interactive games, mazes, questions and answers, and care charts.

Childhood lasts such a short time, but the memories with a pet will last a lifetime.

Gail

Acknowledgment

I would like to acknowledge my family for all their help and words of encouragement while taking the idea for the books all the way to getting them published.

To my mother, who certainly endured some trying years when I would bring home every animal I could get my hands on.

To my children, who are a great inspiration in so much of who I am, and whose father inspired them into becoming the fine adults they are today.

To my husband, for his endless patience on the time I've spent with my own pets. It is not true that the pets eat better than he does!

A great big "Thank You" to each and every one of you.

My Pledge

Being a responsible pet owner, I understand that it takes daily care to be sure that my tortoise gets the care it deserves.

I pledge to give my tortoise food and fresh water every day.

I pledge to never abuse my tortoise. I will never hit my tortoise.

I will never paint or shellac my tortoise's shell.

I pledge to give my tortoise some out of the pen playtime as often as I can, everyday would be wonderful.

I pledge to keep my tortoise's cage clean.

I pledge to read books on tortoises, if I need to find out something about their care.

I pledge to always wash my hands after playing or cleaning up after my tortoise.

Signed,   Date:

_____   _____

Personal Page For Your Tortoise

Your Name _____

Your Age   _____

Tortoise's Name _____

Tortoise's Age _____

Color of Your Tortoise _____

Date Obtained _____

Obtained From _____

Veterinarian _____

Paste a Picture of You and Your

Tortoise Here

Always Wash Your Hands After Playing or Cleaning Up After Your Tortoise
Draw Some Colorful Bubbles!

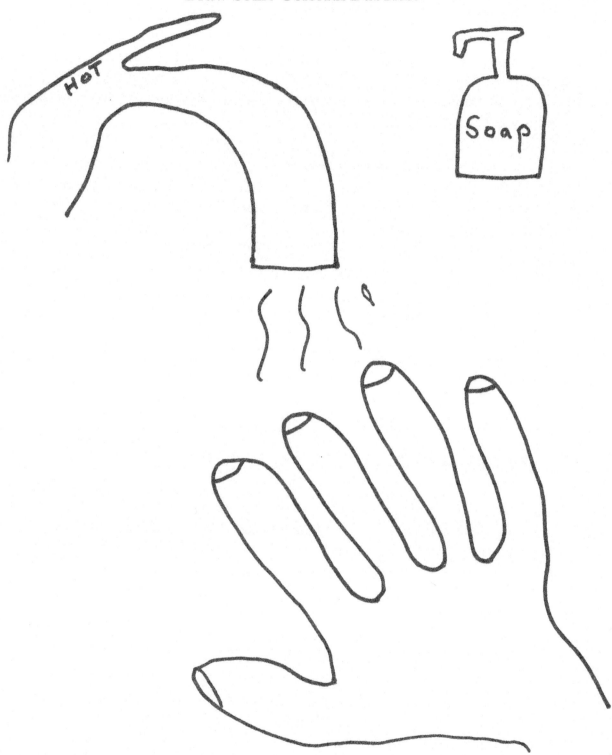

General Information on Tortoises

So you've been wanting a tortoise for a pet. You've promised to take care of it, feed it, and clean up after it. You think a pet tortoise would be fun to have as a pet. Well, I am a tortoise and my name is Shaggy. It takes more than just playing, holding and admiring my good looks to give me the proper care that I need. I'll tell you a little bit about what I like and what you'll need to do to make me happy and keep me healthy.

All in all, I am pretty easy to take care of. Just remember that all my care will fall on your shoulders. I can't get my own water, my own food or adjust the temperature to keep me comfortable. I also need daily exercise and interaction with you. My care will have to last my whole life, each and every day, not just for a few weeks. Are you willing to do this for me? If your answer is yes, then this book will help you to learn how to take care of me.

Here is some general information on tortoises. We'll discuss some of these topics in further detail in the book.

Well, you know that I am in the reptile family.

I am a clean creature and I require a clean home to stay healthy.

My size will depend on the type of tortoise I am. Ranging from a few ounces at birth, to 120 pounds full grown. So be sure to ask how big I'll get, before you bring me home. Even if I am only the size of a deck of cards when you get me, I could have the potential to become very large. Are you prepared for this? Some tortoises get so big and heavy that you might not be able to carry them around.

I like to graze and eat plants.

The top portion of my shell is called a carapace.

The bottom portion of my shell is called the plastron.

I am for the most part, a vegetarian.

I have very strong legs.

I love to dig.

My life span can be extremely long. I may still be around when you graduate from high school.

Did you know that I hatched from an egg?

I live on land.

I cannot swim. So don't put me in deep water.

I do like to soak in a pan of water, be sure my feet can feel the bottom.

I have a good sense of smell.

I also have good hearing.

You will find no teeth in my mouth.

I can be a shy creature towards you until I learn who you are and that you are not going to harm me.

Go slow with me and don't make sudden fast movements or loud noises when you are near me. If I tuck myself up in my shell, don't try to pry me out. Just sit quietly by me and patiently observe how I react to you.

Offering me a tasty treat will sometimes bring me out of my shell.

When picking me up be sure to hold me securely so I don't fall. A fall could crack my shell, or injure my body. You may notice that I sometimes will wiggle to get away or to just get going in a hurry. When my legs are kicking about I may accidentally scratch you. Once I get used to you carrying me around this won't be such a big issue to me. Remember, go slow with me. Tortoises do learn to recognize their owners, especially when food is involved.

When you pick me up don't swing me in circles or throw me up in the air. Never, ever hit me. If you hit me, this will make me afraid of you.

Even a slight tap can hurt or injure me and could even cause me to die.

I like my temperature about 80 – 85 degrees.

I do like to explore. However, keep me away from electrical cords, appliances and other objects that could cause me harm. Sometimes I like to take a little nibble of things to see if they are good to eat. Be careful not to step on me. I am not as slow as people think. If you need to do other things and can't watch me while I explore, put me back in my pen for my own safety. Only take me out when you are able to keep an eye on me the whole time.

My pen can keep me safe from other animals when I am locked up in it. Once I am out of my pen and exploring, be sure that any other pets are locked up in another room so that they don't hurt me. Even with my shell, one pounce from a dog or cat can hurt me. Dogs have even been known to chew on my shell.

Some dogs and cats will except me into the household. However, don't trust any dogs or cats around me if they are not being supervised. It is also a good idea for them to sleep in a different room than me.

While I am out of my pen and exploring, be extra cautious that nobody opens the door that leads out of the house. I might just slip on outside. You can hang a little sign on the door that says, "Tortoise Is Loose" to warn them that I am out of my pen.

The next page has a handy door hanger for you to color, cut out and hang on your door. Decorate the back side of the door hanger too.

Door Hanger

Color this door hanger, cut it out and hang it on the door when I am allowed to have some free time out of my pen.

Make A Backside of the Door Hanger

Questions and Answers

Here are six questions for you to answer on my basic housing and care. You will find all the answers in the previous section on General Information on Tortoises. Read it as many times as you like.

Can tortoises swim? _____

Do I like to dig? _____

Can I sleep with the dog or cat? _____

Do I have teeth? _____

What temperatures do I like the most? _____

Do I need fresh, clean water everyday? _____

I hope you got all the answers correct.

Word Find

Below is a word find puzzle. Can you find the following words in the puzzle? Circle the words and check them off the list when you find them.

___ TORTOISE

___ CAGE

___ SHELL

___ TAIL

___ CLAWS

___ TONGUE

___ SUNSHINE

___ SHADE

___ HIDE

___ WATER

___ COLOR

___ FOOD

B	N	D	V	F	O	O	D	R	P	F	A	S	M	M	H	I	D	E	Z
M	H	S	R	A	C	B	I	T	S	B	F	U	R	A	W	A	T	R	E
U	S	A	A	G	H	J	U	M	P	E	E	N	C	T	A	M	S	A	Q
S	H	E	L	L	W	F	R	U	P	V	A	S	S	T	T	W	A	T	C
I	E	M	P	P	L	E	M	H	O	V	S	H	A	D	E	E	H	O	A
C	D	O	X	I	O	P	R	R	A	C	C	I	A	S	R	J	H	N	G
O	A	N	S	J	E	R	T	Y	U	B	I	N	N	Y	B	A	B	G	E
L	H	O	P	V	B	V	C	A	E	A	S	E	R	S	U	N	N	U	R
O	I	T	N	T	G	H	K	A	C	A	R	R	B	Y	W	R	X	E	O
R	J	U	P	P	Y	O	L	O	V	U	W	A	T	A	I	L	S	I	N
B	C	L	A	W	S	R	B	E	C	T	O	R	T	O	I	S	E	O	N

My Shell

My shell is very unique. It will grow throughout my lifetime. It will help protect me from many dangers.

The upper part of my shell is called the carapace, and the bottom portion is called the plastron.

You must never paint or put any type of household chemicals on my shell. Do not put finger nail gloss on me either. I'm fine just the way I am.

Tortoise shells come in all kinds of colors and patterns.

Tortoises need calcium in their diet to ensure good shell growth and for their bones.

If my shell starts to feel soft, it could be either from a lack of calcium or from not getting the proper amount of UV-B lighting. You can read more on the proper use of lighting and heat lamps in the section called Lighting and be sure to read about Healthy Foods To Feed Your Tortoise.

Don't drill a hole in my shell in order to chain me up!

You may see a few pieces of my shell that has fallen off. This is normal and the pieces are called scutes. When they fall off, you'll see the new scute has grown in where the old scute has fallen off.

I can get an infection in my shells. This is mostly caused by living in a dirty environment. That is why it is important to clean my pen daily and to change my substrate on a regular basis. If I get an infection you will need to have me treated by your veterinarian with antibiotics.

Other reasons I could get an infection are due to injuries to my shell. Maybe the dog did bite me. Or if I get dropped or something has fallen over on me and damaged my shell. Wounds will make bacteria easy to enter my shell.

Color Me

Draw Me A Shell

My Pen

My pen is very important as this is where I'll spend the majority of my time. It will keep me safe and give me a home of my own.

When buying my pen you'll be able to see lots of them at the pet store to make your decision. Some people like glass aquariums and others like a wire cage. Ask at the pet store to see what they recommend for your tortoise. Try to get me the very biggest pen you can. You'll have to take into account the space that you have at home where my pen will be sitting. You might also want to be able to move my pen from different locations. So you'll want to get one that you can handle and transport easily. Some people like to get two pens, one for my main home and a small pen or crate for taking me to the veterinarian, a short car ride, to take me outdoors or for taking me back to the pet store to pick out a new tasty treat. I really like the idea of going to get another treat with you.

The small pen or crate can also be used to put me in while you are giving my big main pen a thorough cleaning. This will keep me from slipping away and getting lost or hurt.

Do not set my pen in direct sunlight that is coming through a window. This can make my pen too hot for me. I like the temperature between 80 and 85 degrees. Also make sure that the air conditioner, fans or the heater are not constantly blowing on me. Keep my pen away from drafts too.

Be careful what you set my pen next to. If I am too close to your curtains, cords, plants, books or other objects, I just might try to pull those into my pen and see if they are good things to eat. I'm sure you don't want to tell your teacher that your tortoise ate your homework.

If you purchase a cage or a glass aquarium, it is ideal if it has an enclosed top, especially if you have other pets, to help keep them out.

Be sure the pen is also tall enough if you have more than one tortoise. We will sometimes climb on each other's shells and could easily grab the rim of the pen with our front claws and pull ourselves up and over.

Tortoises also need a few places to hide under such as logs, or boxes, and to find a shady spot if we get too hot. So be sure that these hiding boxes or logs are not too tall, in case I might climb on top of them and escape.

You will need to supply me with a fresh bowl of drinking water everyday. Be sure to give me one that is really heavy so I don't tip it over and spill out all the water. The pet store has some water dishes, made to look like rocks.

A nice flat food dish will keep my food clean, while I am eating it.

A thermometer is handy to have in my pen. Be sure it is up out of my reach so that I can't bite it.

That should do it for my basic living arrangements. I don't need too much, but setting my pen up correctly will keep me happy, healthy and safe.

Substrate

The other item you'll need for my pen is substrate. This is not only for me to walk on and lay down on, but it also absorbs moisture and odors. Put a small layer of the substrate over the bottom of my pen.

The pet store has substrate made especially for me. Don't use old newspaper or magazines as the ink is not good for me and you know I'll be chewing on it. Some newspaper inserts have staples in them, and these will be deadly to me if I should eat one. Plus newspapers don't take care of the odors that I leave behind when I use the restroom.

Be sure to clean my pen daily by taking out any wet or soiled substrate, and completely change all the substrate at least once a month. You may need to change it more often if I have other tortoises that I am living with. Let your nose be your guide. If my pen smells, it needs cleaning. Begin a good cleaning schedule right from the start of bringing me home.

Scrubbing my pen is also important. It keeps it clean and reduces odors that no one likes to live with. The pet store has cleaners that are made especially safe for use around me. Don't use bleach or other harsh chemicals. These can give me respiratory problems and irritate my eyes. Be sure my pen is totally dry before putting fresh substrate or me back in.

Lighting

When you are setting up my pen for me to live in, you'll want to consider some lighting. Plain old light bulbs will light up my pen and remit some heat. Not just for you to see me, but I will also gravitate to the bright light. This warmth is good for me. I also need another correct type of special lighting that is needed for me to grow and to stay healthy.

This special lighting is called UVB. It stands for Ultra Violet B. You can get these lights and bulbs at the pet store.

I need about 10 to 12 hours of good UVB lighting each day. The bulbs are easy to use, especially if I am indoors the majority of the time. A natural source of UVB comes directly from the sun.

The distance from my shell to the UVB bulbs should be about 8 – 10 inches. Be sure you hang or attach the lighting fixture so I can't knock it down. Broken glass or bulbs of any type in my pen can cause me to get cut, and would be horrible if I should eat or even take a bite of it.

If I don't get the proper UVB lighting, I will develop a soft shell. I also need this lighting to help me absorb the calcium in my diet. Calcium is important for my shell and my bones.

Put both the plain light bulbs and the UVB lights on one end of my pen. I will be drawn to the bright lights and the warmth, and in that way I'll be sure to get the UVB lighting at the same time.

Be sure to offer a good hiding spot within my pen, so that I can cool off and get away from any excess heat.

This is where a good thermometer for my pen comes in handy. Check it often to see if I need to warm up or cool down. Check the temperature at both ends of my pen. Many factors will determine how to regulate the temperature. A lid will keep things warmer, and if my pen is large it will enable me to get to a cooler area, away from the heat, or go back to the warm area.

Healthy Foods For Tortoises

My diet will depend on what type of a tortoise I am. We are for the most part herbivores. We like to graze and eat plants. Depending on where in the natural wild we would have come from, will depend on what we are able to find and eat. Some tortoises will find weeds and grasses to graze on. Other tortoises may need hay and cactus more in their diet. Different parts of the world has different types of vegetation, some are more succulent, others are more dry. This vegetation changes through the seasons as well.

Research what type of tortoise you have and adjust the feeding to be sure you are supplying all the necessary foods needed to keep me healthy. Different tortoises need different types of diets. As an example, Sulcuta Tortoises eat timothy hay, cactus and certain flowers, weeds and grasses. They should not be fed a diet of veggies and fruits. This is why you need to know what type of tortoise you have. Even though we all have a shell, and are classified as tortoises that doesn't make us all the same or needing the same foods to keep us healthy.

Remember your pledge on reading other books to find out more about my care. Researching my needs will be a lot of fun.

Check at the pet store for a specially prepared tortoise food that will be good for me. Most of these foods have many of the necessary vitamins and minerals that I need. However, it is recommended to not rely solely on these prepared foods as my only or main diet. Use these more like a treat than my normal daily rations. I like fresh plants and the more varied my diet the better off I will be.

You can also buy a package of assorted seeds to plant. These are prepared especially for the type of tortoise you have. Then I can crawl through this paradise of fresh plants that you have grown just for me to eat. This is more like my natural food environment and I'll have fun eating these. If you have the room in your backyard or on your deck or patio, make me two small pastures using this special blend of seeds. Then I can eat in one area while the other one continues to grow. Then just switch me back and forth as the plants grow.

These items can be given to most tortoises as a special treat. But a grazing diet of grasses and weeds is best for most tortoises.

Hibiscus
Kale
Spinach
Zucchini
Squash
Carrots and the tops
Peas
Dandelions
Grasses
Leaves
Beet greens
Turnip greens
Prickly pear
Endive
Poppy
Rose flowers and leaves
Many types of weeds
Hosta

Feeding me the proper diet is essential for my shell and for me to grow correctly.

What Not To Feed Your Tortoise

Some plants should not be fed to your tortoise. Here is a list of things that I should not eat. Please take care of me and don't feed me these foods or plants. Many will make me ill and possibly kill me.

Lettuce is mostly water and adds no nutritional value for me.
Cabbage
Corn
Milk
Meat
Oleander
Chocolate
Soda Pop
Mushrooms
Chinaberry
Dog food
Cat food
Celery
Cheese
Bread
Donuts
Poinsettia
Mistletoe
Caffeine
Bird seed

Vitamins & Minerals

Tortoises need calcium in our diets to ensure our shells grow properly. You can buy some calcium dust at the pet store to sprinkle on my food.

If you are feeding me a good well-balanced diet, I may not need any extra vitamins and minerals unless I have been sick for some reason.

If I have been ill, your veterinarian will instruct you on how to give me any extra vitamins or minerals to make me better.

Never feed me your vitamins. Those are for people and they could make me very sick.

I know you are aware that I do need fresh water everyday and I appreciate you taking care of that for me.

Questions and Answers on Food

Here are a few questions for you to answer on what foods to feed me and what foods I should not eat.

What foods will make up my main diet? _____

Are dandelions and weeds good for me? _____

Can I eat mushrooms? _____

Should I have soda pop? _____

Chocolate sure smells good. Can I eat chocolate? _____

Can you name a food that is not good for me? _____

I hope you got these questions correct.

Food is an important part of my day. Eating the correct foods will keep me happy and healthy. I know you are in charge of feeding me correctly.

Soaking

Oh, this is fun. Tortoises need to soak about twice a week in a very shallow pan or tub of water.

This keeps us hydrated.

It also helps relieve any constipation that I may get.

Be sure the pan is large enough to go completely around the outside diameter of my shell, and maybe a little larger so I can walk around in it.

Do not fill the pan with water that is over my head. I can't swim. Only put enough water in just to cover my legs. My head should always be above water.

Once I am in the water, you may see me take a drink. I may also use the pan of water to go to the bathroom in. It is a very good idea to get me my own pan, just for this purpose.

Don't add any bubbles or soap to my water. Plain water is what I want and need. Remember, I will also drink from this water and soap will make me very ill.

If your veterinarian wants to add some medicine to the water for some reason, that will be okay. Follow their advice to help your tortoise get well.

If you use a pan that I can get in and out by myself, you can put my soaking tub right on my tort table, which I will tell you about next.

Tort Table

Having a tort table is a lot of fun. It is basically a nice play area for me to explore and for you to observe me, without having me loose exploring through your house or room.

Tort tables have sides high enough so I can't crawl over them. This will prevent me from walking off the table and getting hurt. You can make a tort table or buy one.

Tort tables are also great for when the weather gets cold outside and I am stuck in the house.

My table will have some of the same items that my main pen has. I'll need some lighting and of course a few places to hide under.

Instead of putting down any substrate, you might try brown craft paper or butcher paper. This is easy to dispose of if I happen to use the restroom on it, or if I get it wet after climbing out of my soaking pan. You can even use old newspaper, but watch me close to be sure I don't try to eat it.

Then add my pan for soaking.

This is a good time for you to check me over for any problems. Look at my feet, my tail and my shell. See if there are any cuts, scratches or sores on me. Are my eyes clear? Do I have a runny nose? Spotting these ailments while they are small is easier to remedy and fix.

Be careful of any cats or dogs that may try to jump onto the tort table to get me. Tort tables typically don't have any lids or covers, so I am not as well protected from other animals.

Giving me a special treat while on the tort table is something that I would like too.

Here is a group of 5 tortoises to color

Taking Your Tortoise Outdoors

Tortoises enjoy the outdoors. The heat from the sun feels good and is very good for our shell and bones.

Be sure that I have cool water to drink and some shade from the sun. A good box to hide under would be ideal too.

When taking me outdoors be aware of any dangers that might be there.

Make sure I can't walk into a pond, creek, lake or swimming pool. I can't swim. So any of these bodies of water will be bad for me.

Keep a close eye on me to see what I am grazing on. Watch for cut pieces of glass, plastics, balloons, nails, rocks and other things that you know are not good for me to eat. Tortoises will just about pick up anything to see if it tastes good.

Any loose dogs in the area may try to get me. Keep a close watch for them.

Be aware of any birds of prey that you have in your area. Eagles, falcons, hawks and even owls. As well as wild coyotes, foxes, raccoons, skunks etc.

If you see any danger in the area, it would be best to take me back indoors to my safe pen or to my tort table.

Making a safe grazing area for me outdoors which would be completely enclosed would be great. Then I can walk and graze and enjoy the sun and my outing.

Be aware that some animals will try to dig under my enclosed pen. The best way to know that I am safe is for you to stay with me while I am out grazing and enjoying myself. Pull up a chair and watch me. I am very entertaining and would love to make you smile.

Tortoise Maze

Tortoises like carrots. Can you take a red crayon and help this hungry tortoise find the carrot through the maze? Then will you take an orange crayon and help him find the dandelion?

Tortoise

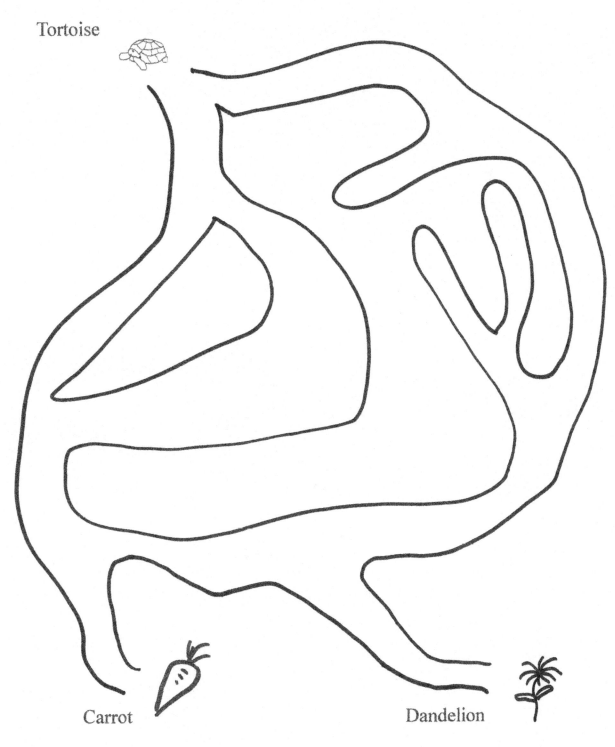

Carrot

Dandelion

Draw Some Scutes on My Shell
Then color me in your favorite tortoise color

Hibernation

Most tortoises will hibernate in their natural habitat. Not all tortoises are capable of hibernating. Pet tortoises that are kept in captivity should not be made to hibernate and some can't actually hibernate because of the living conditions they are in.

First off, your home is not normally cold enough to let a tortoise hibernate safely.

Tortoises will not hibernate if they are in a warm climate. Tortoises will need a cooling down period, prior to hibernating.

Tortoises also need to fatten up before they attempt to hibernate. This fattening up will help them use their stored resources so that they don't starve to death or suffer from dehydration while hibernating.

Sick tortoises should never hibernate and a tortoise that has been ill, but is making a recovery should also never hibernate.

Many tortoises have died when trying to hibernate, so leave this to the professionals and zoo keepers.

In general, pet tortoises should not hibernate. First time tortoise owners will need to care for their tortoise year round.

Captive Bred Tortoises

The best place to purchase your tortoise will be from either a tortoise breeder, a pet store or from a tortoise rescue group.

These places will also be able to tell you about how old your new tortoise is, what it has been eating, what type of tortoise it is, how friendly it is and they will be able to answer all of your questions about your tortoise.

It is not a good idea to take wild tortoises out of their natural habitat and try to make them into a pet.

Wild tortoises are much more skittish and afraid of humans. Many wild tortoises are also protected by the law, and you are not allowed to own one.

Captive bred tortoises are more used to humans. Being bred in captivity they have been accustomed to getting their food from humans.

Once a tortoise has been bred in captivity, it should also never be turned loose into the wild. This is also against the law in many places.

Many tortoises will die if turned loose into the wild.

Health Issues For Tortoises

Tortoises can have a few health problems. Most of these problems come from how the tortoises are raised, what they are fed and in what conditions their housing is in.

A dirty pen will bring on all kinds of health problems.

The wrong types of foods will also cause problems.

No UVB lighting will cause shell and bone problems.

If you see that your tortoise has a runny discharge from his nose or mouth, he may have a respiratory infection.

Shell rot is caused by bacteria.

Soft shells can be caused by a calcium deficiency or from no UVB lighting.

Tortoises can also get internal parasites such as pin worms, hookworms and roundworms. Your veterinarian can check for these parasites.

External parasites include ticks and mites.

Any wheezing or coughing should be checked out by your veterinarian as soon as possible.

If your tortoise suddenly is not interested in eating or refuses to walk, be sure to have the veterinarian take a look at him.

Keeping me from getting many diseases is the direct result of providing me with the proper care I need.

Missing Vowels

Here are more puzzles that you can do. Fill in the missing vowels from the words below. Some of the words pertain to what tortoises like to eat and do, and the last two words are what your tortoise should have plenty of when he is outside.

Use these vowels: A – E – I – O – U

T _ R T _ _ S _

T _ _ L

C R _ W L

S H _ L L

B _ S K

_ _ T

T _ N G _ _

H _ D _

S K _ N

S L _ _ P

C _ G _

P L _ N T S

S H _ D _

W _ T _ R

Word Find

Below is a word find puzzle. These words all pertain to tortoises, and you can find them in the section called General Information on Tortoises. Circle the words and check them off the list when you find them.

___ CLEAN

___ TORTOISE

___ ACTIVE

___ REPTILE

___ GRAZE

___ LAND

___ DIG

___ HIDE

___ SHELL

___ HATCHED

C	T	T	O	R	T	O	I	S	E	L	G	U	I	N	N	M	O
H	A	F	R	E	Q	E	A	R	S	K	S	L	A	N	D	L	O
A	M	F	A	C	T	I	V	E	O	R	E	F	R	A	T	S	P
T	E	R	M	G	I	C	D	O	R	E	P	T	I	L	E	S	U
C	J	I	S	Y	T	L	F	D	V	B	S	A	R	G	U	O	N
H	I	H	W	Q	S	I	A	C	D	G	C	D	I	G	B	S	J
E	U	G	U	I	N	M	A	P	I	G	J	W	F	A	Z	X	X
D	M	T	M	V	K	B	J	Q	W	R	O	D	E	N	T	T	Y
G	R	A	Z	E	F	U	L	A	N	W	C	L	E	V	E	R	W
S	H	E	L	L	S	B	C	A	X	S	Z	O	A	H	I	D	E

35

Color Me

Daily Care Chart

Below is a chart to help you remember to take care of your pet tortoise.

You may want to make some copies of the chart, before you start to use it. Then you'll have plenty for the year and you can hang it someplace where you'll see it to remind you about my daily care.

Put a little smiley face, star or check mark each time you have taken care of my needs.

Keeping me properly fed and clean will make me happy and healthy.

Be sure to clean the area outside of my cage too. Just in case I've kicked some waste, bedding or food out. This will prevent ants and other bugs from coming, and help to control any odors.

	Sunday	Monday	Tuesday	Wednesday	Thursday	Friday	Saturday
Feeding							
Watering							
Playtime							
Clean Daily							
Clean Weekly							

Make Your Own Note Cards

On the next page you will find two different pictures for you to make your own note cards.

Carefully tear the page out of your book. Cut on the dotted line and trim the edge that was torn out of your book.

Fold the paper in half.

Color the pictures and add any flowers, trees, clouds, the sun, etc.

Add your own wording on the inside, such as, Happy Birthday, Get Well Soon or whatever else you'd like.

Give the note card to someone special.

Made For You By:

Made For You By:

Make Your Own Bookmark

Below are three bookmarks. Cut out and draw your own Tortoise on one end and color them in nice bright colors for your books. If you cover them with clear mailing tape, it will make them sturdy.

I Love My Tortoise!

I Love My Tortoise!

I Love My Tortoise!

After you cut out your bookmarks, draw or write your name on the back sides before covering them with tape.

Other Books in the Series

When you need other animal care books with fun activities, ask for these books from your favorite bookseller.

I Want A Pet Chinchilla	ISBN: 978-1491274415
I Want A Pet Hamster	ISBN: 978-1491274286
I Want A Pet Rabbit	ISBN: 978-1491273630
I Want A Pet Guinea Pig	ISBN: 978-1491273968
I Want A Pet Ferret	ISBN: 978-1491274118
I Want A Pet Rat	ISBN: 978-1491274224
I Want A Pet Tortoise	ISBN: 978-1492303275
I Want A Pet Turtle	ISBN: 978-1492303312
I Want A Pet Parakeet	ISBN: 978-1492303350
I Want A Pet Parrot	ISBN: 978-1492303398
I Want A Pet Cockatiel	ISBN: 978-1492303435
I Want A Pet Iguana	ISBN: 978-1492303473
I Want A Pet Bearded Dragon	ISBN: 978-1492303541
I Want A Pet Chameleon	ISBN: 978-1492303633
I Want A Pet Gecko	ISBN: 978-1492303701
I Want A Pet Lizard	ISBN: 978-1492303732
I Want A Pet Snake	ISBN: 978-1492303800
I Want A Pet Betta	ISBN: 978-1492303855
I Want A Kitten	ISBN: 978-1492303886
I Want A Puppy	ISBN: 978-1492303916
I Want A Pony	ISBN: 978-1492303954

Made in United States
North Haven, CT
10 December 2021

12407659R00030